The Width of a Vibrato

Edith A. Jenkins

Pennywhistle Press
Sante Fe
1990

Cover photograph by Lynda Koolish
Design/typesetting by Jabula Publishing
Cover Design by The Groot Organization, San Francisco

Printed in the United States of America
by Cloud Bridge Printing, Santa Fe

ISBN: 0-938631-10-1

For additional copies, address orders to: Pennywhistle Press
P.O. Box 734
Tesuque, NM 87574

Contents

Introduction

Edith Jenkins was born in San Francisco in 1913; she is descended from the merchant Jews who arrived here early in the last century. Jenkins' involvement in anti-war activities and the Old Left began during her student years at the University of California in Berkeley. Since then, the majority of her considerable energy has been devoted to political activism, child rearing and teaching. She is still active — in demand as a board member and also as a member of a huge intense extended family. Her first book, *Divisions on a Ground,* appeared in 1986.

I'm making a point of Jenkins' engaged life because her poetry is so elegiac and contemplative. Often her poems begin with a pang of loss, a pang dwelled on until it passes into the affirmation that expression can provide — not conclusion or resolution, not solace at all, but the assertion of love and grief we might read on a grave marker, whose author wanted her words *cut in stone.* It makes a fact of poetry, palpable. Here's the last stanza of "Scimitar curve of the coast:"

> I want to sing, *Where e'er you walk,* my voice
> rising, *cool gales shall fan the glade.*
> I want to sing, *I attempt from love's sickness*
> *to fly in vain.* I want to sing, *Lullay,*
> *lullay, the faucon hath borne my love away.*

The rush of quotations bears out the idea that poetry can "store" emotion and lodge it with other memories against a day of need, perhaps to forestall that day. I'm describing a memorial impulse shaped by an analytical intelligence, a strict accounting that takes pleasure in discarding what may be comfortable in favor of what is incontestable. That's why these poems have a graven quality, the truth of the hourglass, the sundial's wisdom: I tread a path by which I shall not return. The age passes with a swift foot. We are dust and shadow — Pluvis Et Umbra Sumus. And she owes a debt to the metaphysical poets, who also tried to bring absence and presence close together: *a bracelet of bright haire about the bone.*

Take the poem "Throwing pebbles at her shadow" whose title recasts a note in Hawthorne's journal. "Throwing" places the body on a familiar/strange axis. The poem begins "The fact is herself," followed by three examples that contradict the statement. The poem's logic can encompass memory and association. First: her wavering reflection, which she *wants* to distort, saying, "I wish...that the edges would sometimes fray, the neat circumference abrade." So there is an attraction to estrangement, a will to see its operations. To bear this out, the narrator jumps pronouns from *I* to *she*. "She" scars her reflection with a stone. A romance with estrangement — the second example is a memory of infatuation whose only form of expression was to write her lover's name in a foreign language. Then Jenkins returns to a reflection — to a mirror — but now even she can't translate the image which has taken on the strangeness of the other. Her face can't be deciphered as she tries to read it in a foreign tongue.

"When they told us cancer" also explores presence and absence; it is a work of enormous tenderness. The poem calls husband and wife from the future where they will be "ashes perhaps drifting towards each other" so they can inhabit their familiar shapes. "Belly to back. Arms surrounding. You can't go. I believe only in the material, the flesh, and you are here." It calls the couple away from the past, from the fragility of shared memory, the perilous slipping of experience. Then Jenkins does an amazing thing; she records the lovers' triumph over time, triumph over an enemy whose measure she has taken in poems of great beauty. "The future with its blandishments but more important with its threats is dead." When the past and future are banished, the present "is guiltless, it is ours, it is so boundless, and it is so abounding in love that I am, yes, strangely happy and confounded in the day of our loving."

Robert Glück
San Francisco
Autumn, 1990

Throwing pebbles at her shadow or reflection in the water —

It is, however, after the fact. The fact is herself. Impermeable. And in a way impervious. The stone ripples the water so that her sweater is pleated horizontally across her breasts. Her hands agitate in an excess of fingers. She thinks of herself in an accident. Features erased. After a time the water lies quiet.

On the bank the grotesquerie of an oak tree. Five black ants scurrying. Poppy and wild purple lilac. "I wish," she says, "that the edges would sometimes fray, the neat circumference abrade." She takes a flat rock and skips it in the stream. It climbs her reflection vertically like a scar.

> I remember street lamps. How they claim their own circumference. And the man with the long pole who would light gas lamps at dusk. I remember Dan's poem: *Light bends the edge of darkness back/Where street lamps are/When all around is black...* I used to write *Dan Norton* in Greek script so that the girl sitting next to me would not be able to read what interspersed the lecture notes. When I read it back to myself in Roman script, it read *Dav Noptov.* But that was the only possession. He barely knew me.

Sometimes in the mirror her hair becomes two black parentheses, her brows become two circumflexes. She tries to read her face in a foreign tongue.

AN ACCOUNTING 1956–1971

—Alas, we
Who wished to lay the foundations of kindness
Could not ourselves be kind.
—Brecht

Since the day I knew we lied,
say that hope
has been a person on a teetering ladder
say that on that day
earth's gravity was turned off, people spun
into space:
houses and hamlets, courtrooms, lingerie,
leaflets, and yes, endless agenda, barnyards, factories
and workshirts, shoes and lions, diapers and chickens
took off like rockets
say that conscience
is an affliction and that we hope addicts
awake each morning shaking for a fix
to face the long night of day where
death is no longer ritual and ornament
but private colorless lonely.

NOLO CONTENDERE

As the poet, words
so the dancer distorts
the body, the painter
affronts color, the flutist
shatters sound —

meddlers all.
                              The matter-
of-factness of nature,
the built-in obsolescence
of our particular lives,
time-dated, meticulous.

She said, "I write; therefore, I am."

When no words came, she saw
the bookcase with its jagged
skyline and then the binding
of each book — green, red, blue, black—
the lettering on the spine
book jackets ragged or shiny
no two alike

the grained wood of the floor
every plank a history of the forest
a mystery of cell
the narrow planks, the wide ones

the blue rug, the pattern of the Irish weave
blackness of the wool in the intersection
of yarn, how the fringe is snarled
like uncombed bangs

two vases with African lilies
each lily a projectile of yellow stamen
each stamen corked with an orange ball
four yellow petals with orange stripes
down the center, two tangent inner ones
with their Morse code of dashes and dots

a vase with tepid petunia from the backyard
on a brown wood table, their petals
posing for a still life

If the silence within were a silence,
she thought, I would choose it

The whiteness of the page
vibrates in the light
and the page vibrates
like notes too high for hearing

HOSTAGES AND HEROES

As if all living had led up to this—
a slaughter in the hot desert
of beginnings, the sand receiving
its bloody quenchings.

    (or the self-slaughter of an old man
    in the desert seeking his soul, his son)

It all means nothing.
                                Death gives
occasion for heroes, the hungry and debased,
the gaudy gesture, the lewd posturing.

PENCIL SKETCHES OF FOUR WOMEN

I

Don't ever fly an idea with this one. It's
like trying to fly a kite when there's no wind.
She'll ground it right off in the mire of com-
mon sense.

II

She is so accomplished that her very least
gesture is an accommodation of stars. She
draws her bow across strings nearer to music
than music. She moves her paintbrush gaudily
across the indifference of canvas.

III

She puts a pale patina of mothering over all
discriminating hostilities. She is a system
of life supports. Her children breathe through
plastic hoses and eat through tubes. When
she looks in the mirror, she does not recognize
her face.

IV

In the middle of the night she says to her ac-
cusers, "I did the best I knew how to do at the
time." But they spit back, "Ignorance of the law —"
Each day she must rest up for the night's encounters.
She forgives her friends their incertitudes.

FOR A GRANDSON
August 1985

I don't know where you are now
somewhere in a jungle near Managua
planting trees, up at dawn
with strangers older than you by far,
speaking a language you try to remember.

How frightened you were the night
you came to say goodbye. "It's war
down there," you said, and you measured
your new height against your father's,
the strong boy-shoulders stooped
from your fast growth.

I think of you drinking coffee
in the muggy tropical dawn, clothes
mussed from your sleeping bag, your long
wavy hair above the brows, the depth
of your dark eyes (seekers of messages).
Understander. Soul-sharer.

My love for you has been a secret scolding
in the heart. Breaker of promises. Truant.
Pot smoker par excellence. Sneaker of money
from hidden caches.

And now this is a love letter that I shall
not send, telling you *Yes, I have known,*
I know. I hope you know.

Beauty itself as artifact. Not replication
of life, for it is in the absence of beauty
not of course in nature, but in our lives
where we experience such disappointment.

So it is to art, as it turns
failures to shape or gives
to airy nothingness a name,
we turn again:

last night in default of sleep I recited
lines of old poems — gorgeous, rhymed,
accentual.

"More questions and fewer answers," the judge shouted. As he pounded his gavel on the table, the powder from his wig descended on his black robe and left a collar of dandruff. We noticed when he crossed his legs that he was naked under the robe and that his uncircumcised penis, pink and limp, lay to one side of his hairy balls. "More questions and fewer answers," he shouted.

The jury paid no attention to the proceedings. A woman in a flowered house dress, self-belted above her natural waistline, sat crocheting a long ribbon of mottled worsted. Each time she lifted a stitch with the crochet needle, the pink and heavy flesh on her upper arms shook, she bit her lower lip, and adjusted her wire glasses which still remained awry. The juror sitting next to her was doing a crossword puzzle. He had the newspaper folded in half vertically and in half horizontally. The man to his right had one leg swung over the bar that separated the jury box from the courtroom. He was picking his teeth with a shaved down wooden matchstick. "More questions and fewer answers," the judge intoned slowly and quietly this time like a gramophone winding down.

The plaintiff sat next to her attorney to the left of the judge. She cried silently except when the judge spoke, and then she let out long, wailing sounds that ended with three quick intakes of breath like a child that had been sobbing too long. Whenever she cried loudly, the defense attorney across the room pounded on a small kettledrum and kicked the defendant who lay prone at his feet, deep bubbling noises emitting from his mouth. The court reporter recorded in rapid shorthand and continued to write even when no one spoke. About every thirty seconds, she shook her head and studiously erased a line or phrase.

The spectators in the first four rows sat in rapt attention, their eyes glued to the gavel. In the next four rows, the spectators stood up in unison and followed the silent command of the court marshal as he mouthed the words, "Right, Left." Then each one wandered around the courtroom, stopping to tie a shoe lace, pick at a stray hair. A baby sat on the floor pulling at a wet diaper. The marshal moved to the door. "Credentials, please, before you leave," he commanded.

GOODBYE TO A SON

Your face has already left.
It is an itinerary:

    Marron where the flamenco guitarist awaits,
    the small squares of umbrellaed beaches
    on the Tyrrhenian, Florence
    with your namesake, the uncircumcised David,
    and Perugia of the pink marble and the wild,
    scruffy students of law.

I give you names of friends:

    Massimo in Rapallo, Martin
    in Cambridge, Laura and Giuseppe
    in Rome.

The naming baffles distances.

The intransigence of the dead
                    who will neither argue nor concede.
Nor move one day forward from where we left them
when they opted for the dereliction of eternity.

Your older brother is now younger than you,
his birthday a stop sign on the calendar.
In the photograph his hair is dark.
He is about to laugh and you have to imagine
how he rushes to the kitchen, tastes the stew brewing
on the stove, pauses in the living room to say goodbye.

I wish my sister would resent how I have overcome her.
I offer her her place at the table. I woo her
with her old authority, but she is indifferent
and insists that it does not matter.

Once on the beach, wading with pants turned up
but soaked nevertheless above the knee, fighting
the strong undertow of the Pacific, the landscape all sand
and the whirling of water around the posts of my legs.

Ordinarily the legs propel with only the least signal.
I am purposive. Or capricious. I vote at the polls.
I void. Attitudinize. Swagger. And am rarely late
for an appointment.

LATE SONG

If I believed souls would survive
it would be little comfort.
This clumsy cloak my body
is myself, vague but incumbent
full of largesse and trivia,
and you have done it honor.

I, waiting your loud
footstep on the stairs,
know that no soul
exists without that sole,
sandaled and cumbersome,
joyful and obdurate.

Threat of mortality,
sweet smelling ether,
is in the air, irksome
as itching and less permanent.

...but speech alone
Doth vanish like a flaring thing...

I

Silences
so that the soul can conserve
events, move them into its warehouse,
shelve them, date them for use and for discard,
or forever, or with a half-life —
till death do us part.

Silences
the empty ones, the old winery,
three walls remain and the rock chimney,
and all above, sky and the jagged hill and crag
where the stag leapt and fell,
a rattler hissing among stones.

II

Emptying the mind even of its silences
so that it rests upon itself
drifts of silt lift and swirl
like soft dust

(It remembers the chattering of nerves
high incoherency of wires, raucousness,
but as if remembered from afar)

Dust becomes motes drift downward aslant
transparencies sift through the soundlessness
of stars lit by stars vague and spidery
congeries of wonders

WHEN THEY TOLD US CANCER —

The coeval. That which is evil. *We sleep coeval with the happy dead/Who are ourselves, a little earlier bound/To one another's bosom in the ground.* Though with us, it will be ashes perhaps drifting towards each other. The fact that I do not believe in an afterlife. Still I see *a band of angels coming after me.* They are named Ethel and Leo and Ethel and Jacob and Ruth and if they survived death, *O death, where is thy sting?*

The strangest part. Having lived ever in fear of death. Each morning the fear of loss. The re-arranging. The guilt. Inability to let go... *I'll get by/As long as I/Have you...* But I cannot without you. But I can and I must. And now with each day numbered backwards from an unknown date, cherishing each moment so our love seems new, newly discovered, though old. And all the small irritabilities ("Why didn't you, I keep asking, I already told you") all of them vanishings. Like being first in love. All sweetness, but sober now, not mad or driven. From within. Bodies, but less bodies than soul. Though bodies, too, more precious, less confused by passion. More the familiar. You can't go. Your shape defines my own. Belly to back. Arms surrounding. You can't go. I believe only in the material, the flesh, and you are here. Tangible, turning heavily. Or me awake.

The future with its emptiness banished. *Carpe diem.* Not through effort. But there is only the now. Now and the rich, peopled past. Our remembered. Who will share it. Who will remember. The terror of losing it. That time in Orvieto was it: orange corn drying on the sides of houses. At Crater Lake when Davy walked in his sleep and we drew him to us in the sleeping bag, the bear outside growling. Or the night before the demonstration when I said, "I'm scared," and you said, "Everyone's scared. It just matters what you *do.*" It is not this that frightens me, but the memory I can only half pull in and you not there to say, "It was in Lamu. Remember the child whores on the street?" Or that time we didn't have money for the nightclub till G. brought you next week's salary, and we laughed and were embarrassed because we were celebrating the birth of our baby — which one was it — and I still bleeding.~

These things I store. And the ones I half remember. And the vanishing. The future with its blandishments but more important with its threats is dead. There is only the present. And its afterbirth, the past. It is guiltless, it is ours, it is so boundless, and it is so abounding in love that I am, yes, strangely happy and am confounded in the day of our loving.

CARRYING CHARGES

I

Computed annually 18%, last month's charges plus interest. Bankamericard, American Express, even Barclay's. Cancel the card. It's a rip-off. Tell them thank-you but no thanks. From here on cash on the line.

II

The hard fatty lining in the veins. The nose caricatures itself. Ears continue to grow. The restlessness of the mouth, the nostrils' innuendo halt.

III

I am at each moment all that I am: anew each day I spring from whose distracted brow. And, for I bear with me at all times everything learned and everything forgotten, I move slowly these days.

I make almost no errors.

IV

This capsule contains a thousand small granules that will be released at intervals throughout a twelve hour period. It is advisable not to take liquor or any additional medicine unless prescribed by a physician. Or there is codeine, the rush and the soothing. Perhaps a vodka before dinner. Red wine with the meal, but afterwards I am enervated and sad. There is the headiness of friendship at night before a fire. A drive in the country: it is spring, in California a sudden green. On our return we are cross with each other, argue about money, why the house is so shabby.

V

These days I grow amiable with time. There is the watch I wear on my wrist: it has taken to stopping after ten hours. Then there is the one I keep returning to the watchmaker: it is supposed to rewind with the motion of my wrist. The ship's clock below the stairs has a loud tick, but you can disconnect the bells. Sometimes I prefer to get the time on the good music station between the baroque and whatever or on KGO in station breaks on a talk show.

Bat hanging from the rafters
(ribbed wings   rodent eyes)
waits for night
swoops   veers

Skunk in the yard   its smell
squats in the house
pisses in doorways

In the still of the night
all losses   all terror to come
the scream and clash of metal on highway
its human rubble

AT THE DOCTOR'S OFFICE

And all of a sudden, here I am sitting across a table from a strange man. He holds maps of my body, its latitudes and longitudes. He knows its climate and average yearly rainfall. He tells me of impenetrable roads and rivers that run dry. Demographer of my continent, he reads me back to myself till I am a stranger, begging for a night's lodging in the lost privacy of my skeleton.

He has conspired with my body against me. He has lifted its dim signals with isotopes and charted it with skittering electric graphs. He is a divorced parent playing my child against me. He has made him a prodigy who batters the keyboard in mindless runs, who dazzles with idiot trills.

Doctor and body, void your findings on the cloacal oil paintings on the office walls, piss them on the copy of *Life* where Nixon greets the Pope, on the magenta chancre in *Physicians' News* or the ad for a tranquilizer for the aged, shoot them on the framed degree from Up-State Medical School, 1958.

I want to walk out the door, shy and modest, within my own skin — wordless, abrupt, a poor thing, Doctor, but my own.

Scimitar curve of the coast,
the bright lights of Hotel Helios
at night blue on the Tigullian,
houses in Liguria, how above the caffe
awnings, a palimpsest of colors — apricot
and ochre, the huddled Italian pines,
red roofs with curved repetitive tiles,
the church of Santa Margherita a Montici
where Galileo went for comfort.

These things I store
against the dying of friends, blackouts,
my own death parched and miniscule,
the heart beating out its defiance.

I want to sing, *Where e'er you walk,* my voice
rising, *cool gales shall fan the glade.*
I want to sing, *I attempt from love's sickness
to fly in vain.* I want to sing, *Blow, blow,
thou winter wind.* I want to sing, *Lullay,
lullay, the faucon hath borne my love away.*

i.e.

Access to
Caliban, crouched over dank
genitals, hirsute, turd-matted,
reeks of ammonia
(hoards bloodied hawk's wing,
ewe's flesh, boar's ear)
who nonetheless
sorts
hoaxes from happenings,
horror from the event itself

Or as if orgastic with hate
then surfeited, love flowing over
the self, awash,
listless, uncovered.

WINDOWS

In a painting of Judith Shahn,
windows   are blind eyes
turning inward upon a chair,
a table.

In Botticelli's painting of the Virgin,
the Tuscan poplars and the vineyard
appear through the window.

For Keats, windows
become casements opening
on the foam of perilous seas.

Toni's slides of Ireland
show roses trellised against
Dublin's brick houses:
the poverty sheltered
we do not see.

(The nun said they are so poor
so poor   let the priests
not talk of sex for two
whole years   only let them
address the poverty)

In one of Toni's slides
a window opens upon
a room. Her image,
camera and all,
reflected in the glass —
by inadvertence she said.

How a poet says he will banish
ego, or the scientist, the observer.
Oh the revenge of the diminished thing,
how it hovers in spite on the sill,
the sill itself spattered with the white
droppings of birds.

How do you carve an elephant?
You take away a piece of stone and chip away
everything that is not elephant.
—A Cambodian saying

(For Joanna)

The chisel is the brain
and the soft stuff of drift and down
are wafting menageries
motes that fly through the ether

I am all vagueness   I float on old guilts
Broomsticks of vanished witches
goose me skyward

Furniture is fringed
rugs rest but partially on floors
windows meander   gawk sideways
lines unparallel to floor   to ceiling
are a rocking boat

Chip away all that is not elephant
Let the grey gravel bulk its clumsiness
Loom   Look how its stillness
grounds it to earth   how its arced trunk
scimitars air   how it rests on grounding
Look how its bulk holds distances

Oh its sharpness sheds and flakes
the stone of its discovery

VERTICAL BURIAL

Under the boards, the meshing of sticks
my body can neither stoop nor squat. My head,
above the ground, is a cassette of nerve endings.

The first day when I voided I felt the warm liquid
slither down my thighs, cool as it reached my knees.
As it rounded my ankles, it was cooler still.
It settled in my sox.

The second day I concentrated on breathing. My nostrils
would not take air without instruction. Without instruction
the chest would not rise.
                                        I knew if I slept
it would be all over.

The third day I existed only where my head was.
The 120 degrees my eyes could sweep
yielded insects, the blowing of dust,
and, twice, the feet of men.

Today I am an assemblage of particulars.
All day phlegm has stuck between my nose and throat.
My sex is sticky, it clings to itself, to my leg.
Where the left rib cage connects to the spine
something I think is pain signals to my shoulder.
My shoulder is a vise. It clenches my neck cords.
A tape strung in the space between the base of my head
and my ears plays, replays, and plays.

Who prop, thou ask'st, in these bad days, my mind?

Sometimes, I said, I like the sheer ugliness of it,
pressing meaning through a sieve so it comes out
on the other side with the pattern of the grating
stuck to the mesh or gridded when it falls to the bowl.

Sometimes, I said, a baby has forceps marks on the forehead
declaring it was rough and risky coming through
despite all the panting and the deep breathing.
And the baby is no less or more if it lives, that is,
and does not show damage, and we find we are quite
unconcerned whether or not it is beautiful.

That was the time when you suggested I change a line
because it was awkward.

THE WIDTH OF A VIBRATO

But the note itself is there
the pitch varying, however not so much
that we have any doubt, for example,
the violinist is playing an F sharp.

    Have you noticed her hand
    as it rocks though with the finger
    firm on the string? There is nothing
    more beautiful than the left hand
    of a violinist with its armature
    of bones and the strict ligaments.

But this of course is not at all
what I am speaking about:
I am speaking about how meaning
clings to a word, though the word
tremble in ambiguities, and how important
is the word itself while around it
such resonance.